The Feast that Stopped a War

A folktale from Vanuatu

adapted by Walton Burns

textinspector.com

Leveling information	
Word Count	384
Word Tokens	156
Avg. Words/Sentence	8.73
Gunning Fog	6.62
Fleisch- Kincaid Reading Ease	83.41
Fleisch-Kincaid Grade	3.79

all leveling done with textinspector.com

© 2020 Alphabet Publishing.
All rights reserved.
ISBN: 978-1-948492-93-5
Illustrations by @van.illustrator.
Map created by Central Intelligence Agency, 1998, Public Domain

For discounts on class sets, contact us:
Alphabet Publishing • 1024 Main St. #172
Branford, CT 06405 • USA
info@alphabetpublishingbooks.com
www.alphabetpublishingbooks.com

Table of Contents

Before You Read	4
The Feast That Stopped a War	5
Vocabulary	19
Questions	20
Creating	21
Learn More	23
Other Graded Reader Titles	24

Before You Read

Vanuatu is an island country in the South Pacific, near New Zealand. There are 14 major islands where people live and 83 islands total. The islands were formed by volcanoes. There are still volcanoes there today. It is a very beautiful country with many natural resources. Plants grow very easily there and there is a lot of sea life. Vanuatu is an independent country but it used to be a colony of England and France at the same time!

This story is about a chief named Roy Mata. He was a real person. He lived in the 13th century. He really brought peace to the island of Efate. This is the story of how he did that. Even now, people respect Roy Mata in Vanuatu. No one can give that name to their children. His grave is on a nearby island. It was discovered in 1967 and it an international historic site!

Would you like to live on a tropical island? What would your life be like? If you were chief of your country, what would you do?

I'm going to tell you the story of a great feast, a large meal!.
It happened 800 years ago on the island of Efate in the country of Vanuatu.
This great feast brought peace to the island.

You see before there was a great war in Efate. For 150 years, people fought and fought. They fought over food. They fought over land. They fought over everything!

There was a great king, Roy Mata. He wanted to make peace. So he invited everybody on the island to his village.

He said everyone would eat together. So everyone had to bring their favorite food. People came from all over the island

Some brought octopus or crab. Some brought yams or manioc or taro. Others brought coconuts or mangoes or papayas.

In one family,
the father could bring a mango,
the mother could bring a yam.
Their son could bring a fish.

Everybody brought a different food that they liked best.
Now the people arrived at Roy Mata's land.

Roy Mata told everyone to sit together with the people who brought the same food. All the people who brought crab sat at one table

All the people who brought coconuts sat at another table. The papaya people sat together at yet another table.

Then Roy Mata said, "I am making a new law! Look at the people you are sitting with. They are your tribe now. You cannot steal from each other. You cannot kill each other."

"It also means you must help each other. If a coconut person is hungry, the other coconut people must feed them. If chicken person is hurt, the rest of the chicken tribe must heal him".

"If someone from your tribe is attacked, your whole tribe must defend him. Anyone who hurts a member of the chicken tribe attacks the whole chicken tribe. Who will dare raise a hand against 800 people?"

After Roy Mata had spoken, there was silence. Then, everyone clapped. Roy Mata brought people together. He made people part of tribes. He stopped the war.

Then Roy Mata and his family cooked all the food. Everyone ate the food. They talked and laughed. They sang and danced. The feast lasted for 7 days. And the peace of great king Roy Mata has lasted 700 years.

Vocabulary

crab: an animal with a hard shell, 6-8 legs and 2 claws. Many people enjoy eating them.

to dare: to do something other people think is dangerous or foolish.

heal: to help a sick person.

manioc: also called yucca or cassava. Manioc is a bit like a potato.

octopus: a sea animal with 8 legs.

papaya: a sweet, tropical fruit with green or yellow skin and yellow fruit.

taro: a vegetable like a potato but the inside is white and purple. It is more bitter than potato.

tribe: a group of people, usually related to each other who live and work together. The head of a tribe is often called a chief.

to raise a hand: to put your hand up as if to attack someone.

yam: A kind of sweet potato. The inside is orange

Questions

1. What problem do the people of Efate have at the beginning?

2. What is Roy Mata's job?

3. What solution does he come up with?

4. Did his solution surprise you? Do you think it surprised the people in the story?

5. Go to page 9 and see if you can identify the different foods in the picture.?

6. Have you eaten any of the foods in the story? Which ones? What did you think?

7. Which tribes would there be in your class if everyone used Roy Mata's system?

8. How did Roy Mata solve the problem? Do you think it was a good solution?

9. Who cooked the food? Why is that important?

10. We all feel close to family. What other groups are you part of?

11. If you were a leader, how would you bring people together?

Creating

Do you know a story like this from your culture? Is there a story about the beginning of your country? Or a story about a hero who brought your country together? Maybe you can make up your own legend!.

Tell the story to the class or write it down.

Learn More

Vanuatu is a country with an interesting history and a rich culture. Bungee jumping comes from Vanuatu. The country was an important location during World War II. And there's more to know!

You can learn more about Vanuatu from online resources, such as the Simple Wikipedia article at https://simple.wikipedia.org/wiki/Vanuatu.

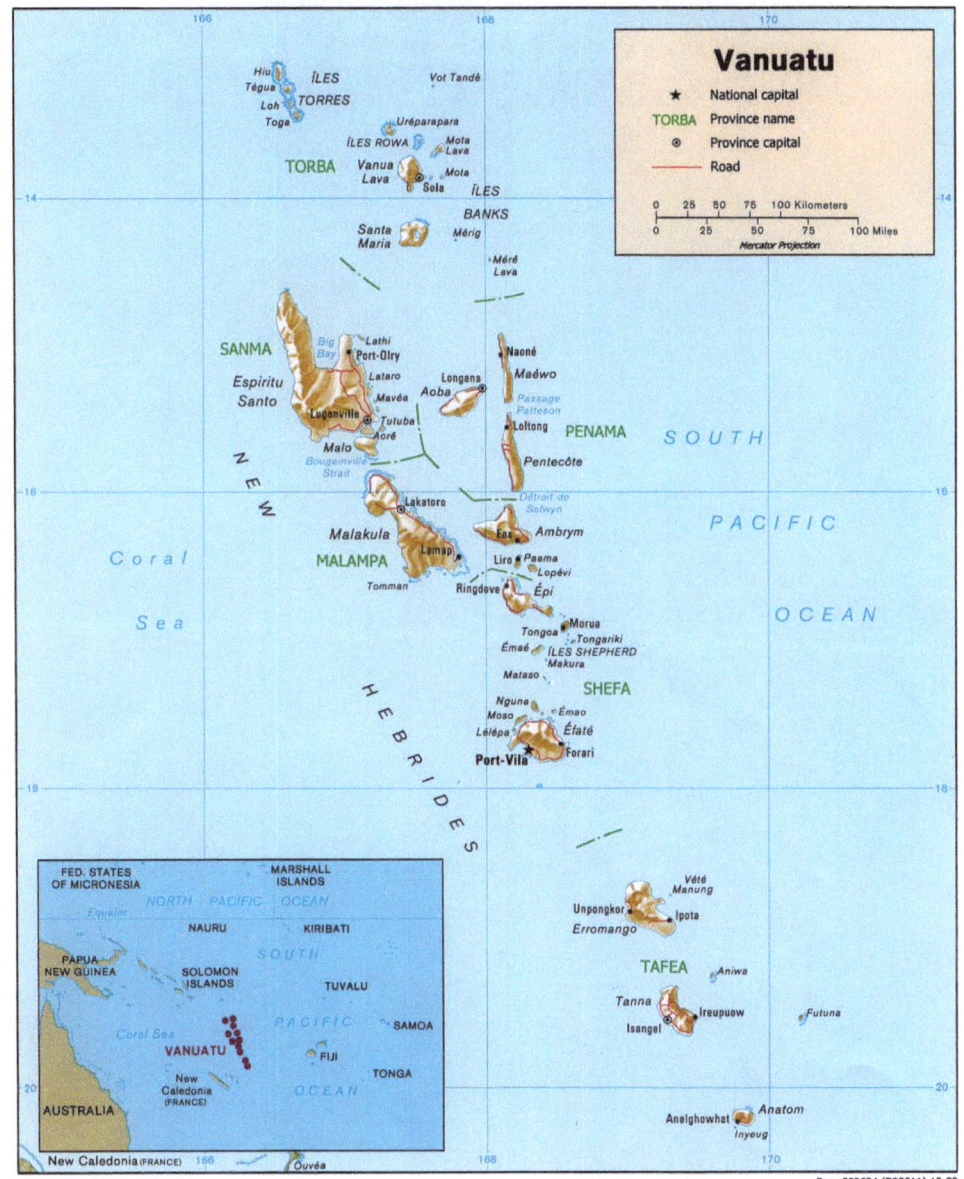

A map of Vanuatu and a small map showing Vanuatu's place in the world.
Efate is the island in the middle of the Y-shape. Port Vila, the capital is on Efate island.

Other Graded Reader Titles

The Real Treasure

The Wise Little Girl

How Babik Cheated Death

The Fox and the Magpie

The Freedom Bird

www.AlphabetPublish.Com/Readers

www.ingramcontent.com/pod-product-compliance
Lightning Source LLC
Chambersburg PA
CBHW040203100526
44592CB00001B/17